On the Job

Teachers

Time

Seth Rogers

Consultants

Colene Van Brunt
Math Coach
Hillsborough County Public Schools

Publishing Credits

Rachelle Cracchiolo, M.S.Ed., *Publisher*
Conni Medina, M.A.Ed., *Managing Editor*
Dona Herweck Rice, *Series Developer*
Emily R. Smith, M.A.Ed., *Series Developer*
Diana Kenney, M.A.Ed., NBCT, *Content Director*
June Kikuchi, *Content Director*
Susan Daddis, M.A.Ed., *Editor*
Karen Malaska, M.Ed., *Editor*
Kevin Panter, *Senior Graphic Designer*

Image Credits: pp.6–7 Frances L. Fruit/Shutterstock; p.8 Amy Couch; pp.18–19 Tupungato/Shutterstock; p.20 Fernando García-Esteban; all other images from iStock and or Shutterstock.

Library of Congress Cataloging-in-Publication Data

Names: Rogers, Seth, author.
Title: On the job : teachers / Seth Rogers.
Other titles: Teachers
Description: Huntington Beach, CA : Teacher Created Materials, 2019. | Includes index. | Audience: K to Grade 3. |
Identifiers: LCCN 2017055025 (print) | LCCN 2018007810 (ebook) | ISBN 9781480759855 (eBook) | ISBN 9781425856915 (pbk.)
Subjects: LCSH: Teachers--Juvenile literature. | Problem solving--Juvenile literature.
Classification: LCC LB1775 (ebook) | LCC LB1775 .R62 2019 (print) | DDC 371.102--dc23
LC record available at https://lccn.loc.gov/2017055025

Teacher Created Materials
5301 Oceanus Drive
Huntington Beach, CA 92649-1030
www.tcmpub.com

ISBN 978-1-4258-5691-5

Printed in China
51497

Table of Contents

A Day in the Life

Mr. Hawkins is a first-grade teacher. He lives in the city.

Mr. Hawkins rides the train to school each day. The train leaves at 7:00. He reads a book on the train.

Let's Do Math!

Mr. Hawkins gets to school at 7:30. Which clock shows when Mr. Hawkins gets to school?

A.

B.

School Starts

Time for school! Students come into the **classroom**. They put their things away. Then, they read on the rug.

LET'S DO MATH!

Students read on the rug until 9 o'clock. Find all the clocks that show 9 o'clock.

A.

B.

C.

D.

Mr. Hawkins loves **sports**. He plays baseball with his class after lunch. Then, they all go back inside for math.

Rules
Rule
#3

The class learns how to read a clock. They learn about **hours** and **minutes**. There are 60 minutes in 1 hour.

Still at Work

There is work after school, too. It is time to get ready for the next day. Mr. Hawkins **organizes** his desk. Then, he checks his students' papers.

3:30

Next, Mr. Hawkins makes copies. He writes on chart paper. He **prepares** for the next school day.

Let's Do Math!

Mr. Hawkins works in his classroom until five thirty. Show the time on an analog clock and a digital clock.

Time to Go Home

Mr. Hawkins walks back to the train. He gets home at 6:30. He loves being a teacher!

Problem Solving

Mr. Hawkins is busy at school. He uses time to plan his day. Draw and write the missing times.

	8:00	eight o'clock
1. 	:	ten thirty
2. 	1:00	__ o'clock
3. 	:	four thirty

Glossary

classroom—a room where classes are taught in a school

hours—measurements of time that equal 60 minutes

minutes—measurements of time that equal 60 seconds

organizes—puts things in order so they can be found easily

prepares—makes someone or something ready for some activity, purpose, or use

sports—physical contests or games in which people compete against each other

Index

Answer Key

Let's Do Math!

page 7:

B

page 9:

A and B

page 17:

Problem Solving

1. 

2. 

one o'clock

3.